COCO&PEBBLES
BATH NIGHT

AF481249

story
Jeremy Wenning

art
Casey Barrett

Coco Publications

Published in 2024, by Coco Publications
Coldwater, OH 45828

Wenning, Jeremy
Coco and Pebbles: Bath Night
Story by Jeremy Wenning; Art by Casey Barrett
ISBN
979-8-8692-9627-6

Library of Congress Control Number
2013935638
Edited by Jon Williams
Book Design by Jessica Vassar
PRINTED IN THE UNITED STATES OF AMERICA

To my wife Vickie and
daughters Brianna and Lauren
for giving me the time to write
these books, and also to
Coco and Pebbles: without their antics,
this book wouldn't be possible.

It was **bath night** for Coco and Pebbles. **We** rounded up some old **towels** as Dad ran the **water.** When Dad **opened** the door, Coco **burst** into the bathroom and **hopped** in the bathtub. He **splashed** water **all over.** Dad was **sopping** wet.

Coco decided he wanted a drink and
began drinking the bath water.
Then he began **splashing** with his **paws**,
getting us all **wet.**

Dad took a large rubber brush and
began scrubbing shampoo into Coco's fur.

Coco enjoyed this so much
he began to lick the air, and I laughed.

After **Dad** rinsed **Coco** off, it was **my** job to **dry** him. But he kept **pulling** on the towel, wanting to **play** tug of war with **me**.

When we thought he was dry, we let Coco
out of the bathroom. He ran into the living
room, rolled over, and began rubbing
his back on the carpet.
I guess he wasn't dry after all.

Then it was time for Pebble's bath.
Dad put her into the tub and soaped her up.
He was just getting ready to rinse her off
when she decided to jump out of the tub.

She slopped **water** and soapsuds all over the floor. **Dad** tried to **catch** her, **but** she was **slippery** with all the **soap** on her.

I came into the **bathroom** to help,
but she **ran** between my legs,
out the door, and into the **living room**.
She rubbed herself **all over** the furniture.

I got a dog treat and lured
Pebbles back into
the bathroom.
I held her in the
bathtub as
Dad rinsed her off.

We came out of the bathroom to help Mom clean up. Coco and Pebbles were clean, but everything else was a **mess!**